Contents

Where sea otters live

Sea otters live in the Pacific Ocean off the coasts of the United States, Canada and Russia.

Sea Otters

Patricia Kendell

HODDER
Wayland

An imprint of Hodder Children's Books

599.7
J

Alligators Chimpanzees Dolphins Elephants
Giraffes Gorillas Grizzly Bears Hippos
Leopards Lions Orangutans Pandas Penguins
Polar Bears Rhinos Sea Otters Sharks Tigers

© 2003 White-Thomson Publishing Ltd

Produced for Hodder Wayland by White-Thomson Publishing Ltd

Editor: Kay Barnham
Designer: Tim Mayer
Consultant: Andrew B Johnson – Programme Manager,
    Sea Otter Research and Conservation, Monterey Bay Aquarium,
    California, USA.
Language Consultant: Norah Granger – Senior Lecturer in Primary
    Education at the University of Brighton
Picture research: Shelley Noronha – Glass Onion Pictures

Published in Great Britain in 2003 by Hodder Wayland,
an imprint of Hodder Children's Books.

Reprinted in 2004

Photograph acknowledgements:
Bruce Coleman 17, 24 (Johnny Johnson);
Doc White 6, 7, 10, 13, 28, 29; FLPA 1 & 20 (Gerard Lacz),
9 (T Leeson/Sunset), 4, 23 (Mark Newman), 11, 14, 19 (Minden
Pictures); NHPA 18 (T Kitchin & V Hurst), 12, 22 (Norbert Wu);
OSF 21 (Richard Herrmann), 26 (Malcolm Penny/SAL),
15 (Frank Schneidermeyer), 25 (Kim Westerkov);
SPL 16 & 32 (Pat & Tom Leeson);
Still Pictures 27 (Chris Martin).

British Library Cataloguing in Publication Data
Kendell, Patricia
    Sea otter. – (In the wild)
    1. Sea otter – Juvenile literature
    I. Title II. Barnham, Kay
    599.7'695

ISBN: 0 7502 4228 0

Printed and bound in China

Hodder Children's Books
A division of Hodder Headline Limited
338 Euston Road, London NW1 3BH

Produced in association with WWF-UK.
WWF-UK registered charity number 1081247.
A company limited by guarantee number 4016725.
Panda device © 1986 WWF ® WWF registered trademark owner.

A sea otter will spend most of its time in the sea.
But its close **relative**, the river otter (seen above),
often comes out on to the river bank.

Baby sea otters

A sea otter mother has one baby at a time.
The **pup** is born in the water near the seashore.

The pup cannot swim at first, but its beautiful, fluffy fur helps it to float. The sea otter mother often wraps **kelp** around her pup to make sure it isn't washed away.

Looking after the pup

A sea otter mother carries the pup on her stomach to keep it safe and warm. She feeds her pup on fat-rich milk to help it grow quickly.

Sea otters do not have many enemies.
But a mother will try to protect her pup
from creatures such as this bald eagle.

Growing up

By the time it is two months old, the pup has learned how to swim and dive underwater.

A mother sea otter teaches her pup where to find food and how to eat it. At six or seven months old, the pup can live alone.

Family life

Sea otters float closely together in the water.
A group of sea otters is called a raft.

Mother sea otters and their pups live together.
Groups of male otters live in groups, away from
the females and pups.

Food

These colourful sea urchins are
a favourite food of sea otters.

They eat many different sea creatures
including shellfish like this crab.

Tools for eating

Sea otters float on their backs and use their stomachs like a table. They break open shellfish using a small rock.

This sea otter is using its teeth
to break open a mussel shell.

Keeping warm

Sea otters have a lot of very thick fur
to keep them warm in the cold sea water.
They do not have a layer of fat like this seal.

Sea otters spend much time keeping their fur clean and fluffy. This sea otter is **grooming** her pup.

Swimming

Sea otters swim using their back feet, which are like flippers. They can stay underwater for several minutes at a time.

They do not often come on the land. When they do, they move awkwardly.

Resting

Sea otters sometimes pull **fronds** of kelp around themselves. This stops them floating away in the moving water while they rest or sleep.

Sea otters sleep with their feet out of the water.
This helps them to stay warm.

Threats...

The sea otter has to **compete** with people who also like to eat shellfish. Fishermen are able to catch a lot of shellfish in one go.

Sometimes sea otters are shot because they take shellfish from **shellfish farms** like this one.

...and dangers

The main danger for sea otters is oil **pollution**. If an otter's fur is covered with oil, the otter gets cold and cannot swim well enough to find food.

Pollution from other dangerous chemicals
can make the sea otters, or their **prey**, sick.

Helping sea otters to survive

People must try to prevent the sea from getting polluted. This is important for all sea creatures.

If people learn more about what sea otters need,
then more of them will survive in the future.

Further information

Find out more about how we can help sea otters in the future.

ORGANIZATIONS

WWF-UK
Panda House, Weyside Park,
Godalming, Surrey GU7 1XR
Tel: 01483 426444
http://www.wwf.org.uk

Monterey Bay Aquarium
886 Cannery Row, Monterey
CA 93940
Tel: 001 831 648 4800
http://www.mbayaq.org

BOOKS

Otter on his own – The story of the Sea Otter: Doe Boyle, Soundprints, 2002

Sea Otters: Bobbie Kalman, Crabtree Publishing 1996.

Lootas Little Wave Eater – an orphaned sea otter's story: Clare Hodgson Meeker, Sasquatch Books 1999.

For more able readers:

Sea Otters(Zoobooks): Beth Wagner Brust, Wildlife Education, 2000.

Glossary

WEBSITES

Most young children will need adult help when visiting websites. Those below have child-friendly pages to bookmark.

http://www.seaotters.org/Kids/
This site has a colouring page and a word search with some interesting sea otter facts for children to learn.

http://www.montereybayaquarium.org/cr/sorac.asp
This site has activities for children, as well as information about the sea otters at the Monterey Bay Aquarium.

compete – to try to win against someone.

fronds – bits of seaweed that wave about in the water.

grooming – cleaning the coat of an animal.

kelp – a type of seaweed.

pollution – when water or air becomes filled with poisons.

prey – an animal hunted and eaten by another animal.

pup – a baby sea otter.

relative – an animal in the same family.

shellfish farm – places in the sea where people raise shellfish.

Index